J Will
Treasures of
Darkness

I Will Give You the Treasures of Darkness

M. Basilea Schlink

KANAAN PUBLICATIONS
Evangelical Sisterhood of Mary
Darmstadt, Germany and Radlett, England

Produced in England by
Nuprint Ltd., Station Road, Harpenden, Herts AL5 4SE

Contents

*I*n the year that King Uzziah died I saw the Lord sitting upon a throne, high and lifted up; and his train filled the temple. Above him stood the seraphim; each had six wings: with two he covered his face, and with two he covered his feet, and with two he flew. And one called to another and said:

'Holy, holy, holy is the Lord of hosts; the whole earth is full of his glory.'

And the foundations of the thresholds shook at the voice of him who called, and the house was filled with smoke. And I said: 'Woe is me! For I am lost; for I am a man of unclean lips, and I dwell in the midst of a people of unclean lips; for my eyes have seen the King, the Lord of hosts!'

Then flew one of the seraphim to me, having in his hand a burning coal which he had taken with tongs from the altar. And he touched my mouth, and said: 'Behold, this has touched your lips; your guilt is taken away, and your sin forgiven.' And I heard the voice of the Lord saying, 'Whom shall I send, and who will go for us?'

Isaiah 6:1-8

Chapter 1

❧

The Nature of the
Holy Trinity

HOLY, HOLY, HOLY, thrice holy is the Holy Trinity and the dwelling-place of God, the throne on high. Yet there is nothing inflexible, remote or abstract about the triune God in His holiness; rather there is life and love in the fellowship of Father, Son and Holy Spirit. In Genesis 18 we read that God appeared to Abraham in bodily form as three distinct Persons. Even so, the Trinity is completely one, for God is one.

When people live in close fellowship, there is warmth, vitality and harmony. Something of the fullness of life can be observed. Yet everything on earth is merely symbolic of what exists in heaven, where there is the one true, divine fellowship of love between Father, Son and Holy Spirit. Here on earth what makes life and fellowship in a family, for instance, so enriching is the love drawing together the members, who are related. This is, however, only a pale reflection of the loving relationship between the divine Persons. Beyond verbal expression, this relationship is hinted at in various passages of

Scripture: 'Father . . . you loved me before the foundation of the world' (John 17:24 RAV); 'Did you not know that I must be in my Father's house?' (Luke 2:49); 'You are my beloved Son; in you I am well pleased' (Luke 3:22 RAV). Elsewhere, too, we sense how the Father delights in the Son, to whom He has given authority over all things: 'You are my son, today I have begotten you. Ask of me, and I will make the nations your heritage, and the ends of the earth your possession' (Psalm 2:7-8).

Could there be a relationship more tender and loving than that of the Father, Son and Holy Spirit? Even in human life it is heart-warming to see how a father relates to his son, and the son to his father — provided it is a relationship of mutual love, trust and respect. What a pleasure it is to hear them conversing in a spirit of sympathy and understanding! Yet this is but a dim shadow of the relationship of the Father in heaven to His only begotten Son, whom He dearly loves.

Who can begin to imagine the loving conversations that must have taken place between the Father and the Son before the foundation of the world? The Father would have unfolded to the Son His plan to send Him to earth for the redemption of the world; or the suggestion may have come from the Son in His infinite love so as to restore to the Father His wayward children. When the Father made known His will, Jesus' response may have been similar to the words in a hymn by Paul Gerhardt: 'Yes, Father, I will gladly bear whatever You have ordained for Me.' At the same time the Holy Spirit would have participated fully in the plan of redemption, for

'Christ... through the eternal Spirit offered himself without blemish to God' (Hebrews 9:14).

With what tender love — we are using human terms — the three Persons of the Holy Trinity may have comforted one another at the thought of the painful separation impending. And with what expressions of sympathy, each seeing only the grief of the other, though the suffering must have been equally great for all three Persons. Everything that the Son suffered on earth, the Father must have suffered in union with Him; otherwise He would not be true to His name Father. When the Son was blasphemed and dishonoured, the Father's glory, present in the Son, was brought low and disgraced. The same is true of an earthly father and son. What happens to one brings credit or discredit to the other. Similarly, the Holy Spirit, who spoke through Jesus, was also grieved when the Son was blasphemed, for Father, Son and Holy Spirit are one, completely one. They are inseparable, indivisible.

How great must be the love binding the Holy Trinity, so that there is perfect oneness. Love is what makes us one. The words 'God is love' refer to all three Persons of the Godhead, and this accounts for the perfect unity of Father, Son and Holy Spirit. But since complete oneness is the hallmark of love, nothing is so grievous as being separated from those so loved.

When the Son, who was at the Father's side (John 1:18), assumed a human body and walked on this earth, far away from the Father's house, what untold anguish this separation must have cost the Father and the Son! Just how much Jesus suffered is evident from His reluctance to leave the Temple in Jerusalem during His visit as a young boy. Although people had turned this house of God into a den of thieves, the Son of God said, 'Did you not know that I must be in My Father's house?' What wistful yearning lies in these words, expressing the deep pain of separation. So great was His homesickness that just to 'touch the fringe of the garment' of His beloved Father was a comfort.

When the Son later ascended to heaven and returned to the Father, what rejoicing there must have been! The joy would have corresponded to the grief of separation. Who would not have wished to be present when love was reunited with love?

The Holy Trinity is holy, that is, perfect. In Matthew 5:48 we read how Jesus challenged His followers, saying, 'You, therefore, must be perfect, as your heavenly Father is perfect.' The perfection of the Godhead consists first and foremost in love — love which knows no bounds, which is not resentful, which does not keep a record of wrongs, which is forbearing, gracious, merciful and full of goodness and forgives all sin. What life must pulsate in the heart of the triune God, who is perfect love! It is a veritable furnace, enveloping the world and the sons of men in a glowing fire of love. But greater still, we may assume, is the love of the three holy Persons to one another. How tender must be the love with which one approaches and addresses the other, and yet how powerful — like a mighty, rushing wind!

What no ear has heard, no eye has seen, God has prepared for those who love Him (1 Corinthians 2:9).

Surely one of the most precious things that God has prepared for His own as a token of His love is the privilege of one day listening to these divine conversations of the Holy Trinity. Scripture says that if we overcome we will sit beside God on His throne and rule the nations with Him, having, as it were, an active role in His divine ministries (Revelation 3:21; 2:26-27). If this is so, should we not also be permitted to listen to the conversations of the Godhead as His redeemed children?

We read in the Bible that councils are held at the throne of God to which the angels are granted access (Job 1:6; 2 Chronicles 18:18-21). Furthermore, it says that we have an even higher position than that of the angels, for we will judge them (1 Corinthians 6:3). We will probably participate more fully in the hidden purposes of God than they do, just as Elijah and Moses, for instance, had foreknowledge of Jesus' death and spoke with Him about it on Mount Tabor (Luke 9:30-31).

What greater glory could there be than being present at a conversation of the Holy Trinity and listening to the voices of the Father, the Son and the Holy Spirit discuss the administration of the universe. If we realized what it means to be counted worthy of attending one such a council in heaven and of hearing even one such conversation, we would stake everything on this hope. The overcomers will 'inherit all things' (Revelation 21:7 RAV), including these privileges. What bliss to be numbered among these victorious souls one day! Abiding at the side of the Godhead, they are privileged to partake of the divine love, as well as sharing in the priestly suffering and intercession of Jesus till the day when God's saving purposes will be fulfilled.

It is a miracle surpassing human understanding that the holy triune God, though sufficient in Himself, should want to draw close to us and to include us in His divine life and love — yes, that He should desire to give Himself to us. And why? As children of the Father, betrothed to the Son and visited by the Holy Spirit, the Comforter, we are to be united in love with the Father and the heavenly Bridegroom and the Holy Spirit.

There in a sinner's heart the Father and Son come to dwell through the Holy Spirit, if awaited with love. As Jesus says, 'If a man loves me, he will keep my word, and my Father will love him, and we will come to him and make our home with him' (John 14:23). Love is the key that opens the heart of God so that we might find access to Him and understand Him. God is love. How else, other than by love, can we come to know Him? And so it is love that draws the triune God to us, to make His dwelling with us.

He comes to a heart where He is loved and where His presence is ardently desired. Only love can grasp the mystery of the Holy Trinity — without love, it remains closed to us and the Holy Trinity is just a vague concept. In the Creed we confess our faith in the triune God, but so often we lack a personal relationship to Him as such. To love is to have a personal relationship to the one we love, taking an active interest in every aspect of his life and being occupied with him alone. Usually we have this personal relationship to Jesus. How our hearts rejoice over His salvation! But is this jubilation equally present when we pronounce the names of the Father and of the Holy Spirit?

Only if we love all three Persons of the Godhead can the Holy Trinity dwell in us. What riches this brings us! Truly, then we have the fullness of life, the fullness of love. God comes to us, as it were, threefold. Figuratively speaking, three streams of fiery love pour into our hearts from the Father, the Son and the Holy Spirit, and yet it is all one stream, for God is one. Is this not heaven? It is as if God were making His home with us, and when that happens there is heaven: the fullness of glory, divine splendour and love. When a person becomes a dwelling-place of the Holy Trinity, there is a breath of heaven about him.

How do we become a dwelling-place for the Holy Trinity? What path do we have to follow for the triune God to reveal His mysteries to us? Have we not all found that when we see ourselves as sinners in need of God's forgiveness, this drives us into the arms of Jesus? Through conviction of sin we enter a relationship with Him, for the sinner and the Saviour, the Friend of sinners, belong together. But the way to the Holy Trinity is not so easy to find, because we sense something of the thrice-holy and in our hearts the words are echoed, 'Woe is me! For I am lost; for I am a man of unclean lips' (Isaiah 6:5).

When we think of the Holy Trinity, we also think of the City of God, of the holy throne, and of a glory so holy that we dare not approach it the way we are.

We recall what the prophet Ezekiel and the Book of Revelation say about the majestic glory of God. In spirit we see thunder and lightning surrounding the throne and hear the seraphim continually call, 'Holy, holy, holy is the Lord of hosts!', making the foundations of the throne tremble with their cry.

Who dares to draw near to the holiness of God? Does not Scripture say that without sanctification no one will see the Lord and that only overcomers may enter the City of God and approach the throne (Hebrews 12:14; Revelation 22:14)?

Jesus accepts sinners. One and all can come to the Saviour and, after bringing Him their sins and receiving forgiveness, experience the grace of redemption. But only those souls who have been purified may approach the throne of the thrice holy divine Majesty: 'Everyone who has this hope in him purifies himself, just as he is pure' (1 John 3:3 RAV). In other words, a certain path needs to be followed if we are to experience the presence of the Holy Trinity. Everyone can follow this path leading to the throne, for free access is granted through the blood of Jesus (Hebrews 10:19). All we need to do is to tread it. What does this mean in practice?

We may find it helpful to consider the tabernacle of the Old Testament and the way from the court to the holy of holies containing the ark of the covenant, which symbolizes the majesty of God's throne. Strangely enough, it was completely dark in the holy of holies. And so by analogy the way to the holy of holies, to the Holy Trinity, is a path leading into and through spiritual night and darkness. In the roofless court of the tabernacle there was light during the day; only at night was it dark. In the holy place, which was a windowless room lit up only by the light from the golden candlestick, it was dark even during the day. In the holy of holies there was no light whatsoever. This is probably symbolic of the holy City where God dwells and reigns and which has no need of sun or moon, for the glory of God is its light, and its lamp is the Lamb.

By means of this symbolism the Bible tells us that only by following dark pathways will we come to the radiant light of the throne where the triune God dwells. Indeed, how will we be capable of enduring the holiness and splendour of the Holy Trinity unless we have first died to self, losing our dubious prestige along dark and difficult pathways? In broad daylight we cannot see the stars. Similarly, we cannot recognize God if we continue in the unbroken strength of our soul, spirit and body. This means that if our personality is displayed in all its natural light and glory, we are incapable of recognizing God, the eternal light. We obscure Him. God chooses that which has been reduced to nothing.

What a long process it is before our own splendour fades away, and before the unapproachable God can begin to manifest His glory in our lives, as in the holy of holies! To use an analogy, that which is brilliant in daylight loses its lustre at night, but it is then that the moon and stars, which we could not see before, begin to shine. Only at night can we admire their radiance and beauty. Likewise, God reveals Himself most wonderfully to the soul when it is in the night and dwells in the 'valley of the shadow of death', the vale of suffering. As Isaiah writes, 'The people who walked in darkness have seen a great light; those who dwelt in a land of deep darkness, on them has light shined' (Isaiah 9:2).

Where else but in darkness can God let His light shine forth? He is the one who once called light into existence when there was total darkness. He has no need of a light, not one single glimmer. Indeed, He would diminish His glory if He were to manifest it during the day and let it blend with our light.

So it is a divine law that God dwells with those who walk in darkness and in the shadow of death. Only in the dark can the human eye see light properly, and only in the night of suffering can the human heart perceive and understand God properly. God, who is the light, and the suffering soul in darkness belong together. In the same way God, who is the essence of strength, and man in his frailty belong together, for does not the Lord say, 'My power is made perfect in weakness' (2 Corinthians 12:9)?

Times of darkness are messengers from the loving Father-heart of God. They are meant to bring us true joy and happiness, a revelation of God, and to prepare our hearts as a dwelling-place for the Holy Trinity. Those who welcome suffering will experience this. The apostle Paul entered the night of weakness, praising God for it, and we see how he was filled with the power and glory of God, writing, 'I will all the more gladly boast of my weaknesses, that the power of Christ may rest upon me' (2 Corinthians 12:9). Elsewhere he declared, 'With all our affliction, I am overjoyed' (2 Corinthians 7:4).

In accepting our trials, in welcoming the night as a helpful friend that leads us into the light of the revelation of the holy triune God, we will discover its blessings. By the working of the Holy Spirit the night will refine our souls of the dross, preparing us to be a vessel of the Holy Trinity.

What is meant by the term 'night'? Believers sometimes speak of passing through spiritual night. But the interpretation of 'night' varies from person to person, because there are different degrees or kinds of spiritual night. Figuratively speaking, there are three regions of the night through which we have to pass before we reach the goal of the holy of holies, where the triune God reveals Himself in His majesty and glory. This in no way implies that after passing through the first or second region of the night, we have left them behind us for good. Because we are sinners to our dying breath, we will time and again have to traverse the first two regions of the night even if — and this is what makes the difference — we have already arrived at the third region and have made our home especially there.

God in His holiness
*   Sweeps over the mercy seat,*
Dwells in His holy place.
Cherubim worship Him,
Seraphim bow to Him,
Hailing His holiness.

Holy is God and true,
Earth pays its homage due
To His great majesty.
And His most glorious light
Sheds holy radiance bright
All through the realm of heaven.

Holiest Trinity,
Dwelling in majesty,
Veiled by the shining cloud!
The Three in One imparts
His love abroad in hearts
That are at peace with Him.

God is the Holy One!
Brighter than noonday sun
Blazes His robe of gold.
Royal divinity,
Holy in majesty,
Ruling the universe.

Holy is God the Lord!
How can He be adored
Truly and worthily?
Humbly before Him bend
Earth's souls from end to end,
Once they His glory know.

Chapter 2

❧

The Night of Guilt

Most familiar to us all is the night we have
brought upon ourselves through our sins. We
will find this night especially dark if, after succumb-
ing to sin, we do not want to admit it before God
and others. Instead of coming to Jesus and those
against whom we have sinned and receiving forgiveness, we keep our sin to ourselves. In our pride
we cannot bear to think that we have failed again,
and it grows dark in our souls.

It is the night of hell we have entered. The effects
are clearly distinguishable from those of the night
that comes from God. The person finding himself in
the night with God radiates peace and kindness.
Apart from those closest to him, no one notices
anything of his suffering. How different from the
person who is undergoing night because of his sin!
He becomes moody, unpleasant, touchy, defiant,
depressed and usually looks sullen and downcast.
That is understandable, for only if we walk in the
light, as God is in the light, do we have loving
fellowship one with another, and only then do
we experience the cleansing power of Jesus' blood
(1 John 1:5-7). But if we do not want to confess our

23

sins and bring them to the light, we will remain in darkness.

We will also remain in darkness if we cannot come to terms with the fact that we are sinners. We may dutifully confess our sins to others while deep down inside we are just annoyed with ourselves for having failed again. Pride keeps us from acknowledging that we are weak, sinful beings, always liable to sin. Ultimately, such an attitude is rebellion against God. Yet if we defy God, we erect a barrier between Him and ourselves, for He gives grace only to the humble. And gradually we find the darkness within growing denser and denser. We may fall into great inner conflict and self-pity, failing to realize that we have only ourselves to blame for the night encompassing our souls.

Inner trials, which we consider to be suffering sent by God, can often be traced back to our sins or, more accurately, to the sin of sins: unwillingness to acknowledge that we are sinners. So long as we refuse to see ourselves as such, we will receive no help. Only the sick, not the healthy, need a doctor.

Actually, our sin should not lead us into the night. Rather it should be the starting-point for us to enter the light, because it drives us to Jesus, to the Father and to the Holy Spirit, whose help the sinner needs. But as doctors, psychologists and spiritual counsellors can affirm, there is much inner night when there is unconfessed, unforgiven sin, which darkens the soul. Sadly, many believers suffer from depression, melancholy and inner turmoil. In their pride, which has acquired a religious coating, they often find it hard to accept the fact that they are sinners and to admit their specific sins and failings. Such hypocrisy doubly darkens the soul.

We need to leave this night behind swiftly, whenever we find ourselves there, for those who linger will be engulfed by it. This region of the night should only be a brief transition. The pain it causes us to see our sins will soon turn into thanksgiving and joy over the forgiveness we have received.

There may be another reason why a person is unable to leave this region of the night quickly, and that is if he deliberately persists in a particular sin, such as a lie, impurity, unwillingness to forgive, slander or malicious gossip. Again, the person fails to realize — especially if he is a believer — that this is very often the cause of the darkness in his soul. He may still attend church regularly, belong to a Christian fellowship, read his Bible and spend much time in prayer. Because he believes in Jesus and calls himself a Christian or born-again believer, it never occurs to him that his depression might be a direct result of his sins.

Only those claiming to be religious could be called hypocrites by Jesus. Today the danger of hypocrisy is just as great. Only believers can labour under the delusion that their lives are in order, because at one point they accepted Jesus as their Saviour and received the forgiveness of their sins. But it is a serious matter if they continue to persist in sin, not bringing their wrongdoing to the light and not repenting of it. In their self-assurance and self-complacency they do not notice that God has withdrawn from them, denying them that revelation of His glory which He gives to those who are going through the spiritual night with Him. As a result they are often joyless, irritable or discontented. In contrast, a person in the night with God radiates joy, peace and love.

However much we talk about the City of God and the Holy Trinity, we will never reach the heavenly Jerusalem, the throne of the Holy Trinity, nor will the Holy Trinity be able to enter our hearts, if in blindness and hypocrisy we persist in sins like those mentioned above. Jesus says, 'If a man loves me, he will keep my word, and my Father will love him, and we will come to him and make our home with him' (John 14:23). This applies to the person who obeys God's Word, above all the Ten Commandments, and patterns his life on the Sermon on the Mount and the whole of the Gospel.

Here the prerequisite is clearly laid out: Whoever wishes to dwell in the presence of the Holy Trinity has to leave this region of the night and get ready to pass on to the second region, the night of chastening.

Chapter 3

❧

The Refining Night
of Chastening

WE ARE ALL ACQUAINTED with this night, and time and again God leads us into it. Even those who have already tarried at length in the night with God will be led repeatedly into this region of the night, for till our dying breath we need to be purified through suffering. We will remain in this region of the night for as long as God wishes to have us there. Nonetheless, the length of our stay partly depends on us and our reactions — whether we resist God's chastening or whether we bear it in patience and even love.

There are various forms of suffering and chastening that God can send us: sickness, bereavement, disappointments in people, loss of earthly goods, all kinds of fears and hardships, as in wartime. But the reactions to suffering when God takes or withholds this or that will vary from person to person. Either we accept God's dealings and humble ourselves beneath His mighty hand, or else we are rebellious or perhaps downcast, which is another form of defiance.

A person can accept chastening if he has learnt to say in the first region of the night, 'I am a sinner. I am at fault. — Yes, this is what I am like!' If he can say that, he will have the right response when chastening comes. It is the response of one who feels constrained to acknowledge his guilt: 'I am receiving the due reward of my deeds. I need these disciplinary measures.' Unless we suffer a disappointment in someone we love or the loss of a loved one, how are we to experience release from those soulish attachments we are all prone to? How can we be transformed into the image of Jesus, the image of humility and meekness, unless our proud and arrogant nature is dealt with by such chastening as slander and hostility? How are we to learn to love if our love has never been tested by malicious or unfair treatment? Humble people, who have come to see themselves as sinners, willingly accept all these disciplinary measures from the hand of God. They persevere in the inner night caused by such chastening.

Darkness surrounds our souls when we have lost a dear one, or when someone we love ignores us, or when we are afflicted with a severe illness that may confine us to bed and bar us from all our activities. Night falls upon our souls when loved ones turn to evil ways, straying far from God, or when they are in great misery and suffering. No one is spared this night. In dealing with our strong emotional drives, which are part of our sinful heredity, God has to apply the pruning knife of suffering. And when He leads us into situations where we face opposition and difficulties, it is to refine our faith. But those who are willing to be trained by such discipline will find that afterwards it yields the peaceful fruit of righteousness (Hebrews 12:11).

Just as in the darkness of the holy place the lamps were lit, allowing one to see the table of the bread of the Presence, the golden candlestick and the altar of incense, all of which typified Christ, so in the inner night new divine light arises. If on pathways through the night and under the chastening hand of God, something in the soul has died and emotional ties have been refined away, a wonderful thing happens: a new, personal love for God springs up and a previously unknown happiness dawns. It is as if the place formerly occupied by a loved one is now being filled by Jesus Himself.

But not for all believers is this refining night a time when special tokens of grace and divine revelation are granted, a time when a great love and devotion to Jesus are born. Many are unhappy for the rest of their lives at losing a loved one or because of someone who caused them immeasurable suffering. Their souls remain in the night, sombre and joyless. Why the difference in experiences? Does it depend on one's personality? No, it depends on one's attitude towards God's chastening, that is, suffering.

Blessing will flow in the same measure that I have lovingly embraced my cross. The night that was brought to me by my cross will be turned to light as it reveals its blessing. God in His love will draw near to the humble person who willingly accepts chastening as his due. Those failing to see a connection between their sin and the suffering laid upon them will remain in a state of darkness a long time or for the rest of their lives. But anyone looking for a connection will find it. There is always a link, for Scripture says that God chastens us so that we may share His holiness (Hebrews 12:10).

Along paths of chastening we are to be purified of the sins and dross in our lives. When we realize that we are sinners meriting chastening, we begin to appreciate our suffering. We can even rejoice in it, knowing that it works for our good by transforming us into the image of Jesus. With this realization the night gradually recedes; the pointlessness of our suffering vanishes; and finally the light of God rises over the night. His glory shines forth, for such times of night are always followed by gracious times of refreshing, bringing us the revelation and nearness of God. New life, love and joy are kindled in our hearts.

It is a spiritual law for the night of chastening and refining suffering: To the extent that a person has surrendered all he holds dear, practised self-denial, and suffered degradation and scorn, to that extent will he be endowed with the Lord's love, enriched and filled with joy. Often he will feel overwhelmed by the wealth of blessings awaiting him at the end of a pathway through the night. Though perhaps weeks or years later, God rewards us for having followed pathways fraught with inner trials, darkness and chastening. How infinitely greater will be the grace awaiting the person who has passed through the third region of the night — the night with God! Surely this must defy description.

On paths of suffering
  When night surrounds me,
I praise the blessing that will come.

I'll suffer gladly —
This will prepare me
To dwell in glory without end.

Suffering will be no more,
For evermore transformed
To light and joy at Jesus' throne.

Chapter 4

❧

The Night with God

GOD WILL LEAD into the night with Him only those whose one response to everything He has brought into their lives is: 'Yes, Father.' We have seen how in the night caused by our own fault, everything depends on this one word Yes, on accepting the fact of our sinfulness, our wretchedness, our failures. This is the Yes of truth and humility. It makes us hasten to the cross and compels us to break with sin. Those who can say Yes will pass swiftly through this first region of the night each time.

Again, we saw that this Yes is required of those in the second region of the night. Each time we have learnt what God wanted to teach us and given our wholehearted assent to chastening, allowing it to purify us, we may leave this second region of the night and God will be able to take us into the night with Himself.

Only those who have submitted to the refining work of the Holy Spirit in the first two regions of the night and have emerged full of light are capable of entering with Jesus the night of the fellowship of His sufferings (Philippians 3:10). Only the purest of lights can withstand the darkness. Similarly,

only purified souls who have been set free from
all self-seeking, all soulish and carnal desires, can
endure the attacks of evil forces in the night with
God; for even hell must yield before the light,
which rebukes it. How important is the prayer of
Gerhard Tersteegen, 'Lord, come dwell within me'!
We should yearn to enter the night with God
in order to become a dwelling-place for the Holy
Trinity in this life. It is so important that we do
not linger in the first two regions of the night.

The night with God is a pure suffering, since
the focal point is God and not us, although this
never implies sinlessness on our part. In this form
of suffering God lets the purified soul experience
something of the fellowship of His sufferings. This
is not a night incurred by our refusal to admit our
sins. Nor is it primarily a refining night, although
a process of refining still takes place during the
night with God. Rather it is suffering for Jesus'
sake. Paul says of this suffering: 'In my flesh I
complete what is lacking in Christ's afflictions for
the sake of his body, that is, the church' (Colossians
1:24); 'Henceforth let no man trouble me; for I bear
on my body the marks of Jesus' (Galatians 6:17).

At this point some may ask with concern, 'Isn't
it the emotionally unbalanced who tend to be carried away, imagining that they are in great spiritual
night because they are sharing Jesus' sufferings?'
Admittedly, the devil is quick to pervert anything
pertaining to the realm of the divine. But the fact
that he tries to discredit the fellowship of Jesus'
sufferings indicates that here is something great
and divine.

Holy Scripture tells us clearly how to differentiate between an emotional person being carried away with thoughts of suffering with Christ and a purified soul enduring the night with God for Jesus' sake. We read, 'You will know them by their fruits' (Matthew 7:16). Though in the depths of night, a purified soul will radiate Jesus, with whom he suffers and who is present in him; whereas the emotional soul undergoing night will exude self-centredness and pride.

A person in the night with God bears the imprint of the heavenly world, because he is suffering with Jesus, who is the very essence of heaven, and for His sake. Jesus is the focal point of his life. In the night of chastening the person, however, is the focal point, since he has to endure the night for his own sake — a great difference. This is why during the night of chastening a great deal of our human nature and sadness surface.

Of course, this does not mean that during the night with God the soul is, as it were, transferred to heaven. On the contrary, a person privileged to suffer with and for Jesus will come under special attack from hell. God gives the powers of hell permission suddenly to touch him with the hand of death. Perhaps a parallel can be drawn to Jesus' experience in Gethsemane, when He was attacked by the hordes of hell, who almost tormented His soul to death, drawing from Him loud cries and tears (Hebrews 5:7) and causing Him to sweat blood. Jesus endured this for us as the pure and righteous One, whereas we suffer the attacks of hell because of our sins and for our purification. But at the same time we share in the fellowship of His sufferings, in order to 'complete what is lacking in Christ's afflictions for the sake of his body, that is, the church' (Colossians 1:24).

Body, soul and spirit can, as we know from the life of the apostle Paul, undergo various trials vicariously. These may be invisible, mystical sufferings or visible ones, such as persecution, martyrdom, or the marks of Jesus' wounds, which were imprinted on Saint Francis of Assisi and others after him. A person may also suffer great darkness and aridity of soul, sometimes feeling as if he were being led into a desert, because God withdraws His comfort and the sense of His presence. Indeed, there may be times when the soul undergoes a manifold dying process. It is as if the hand of death were reaching out and nearly suffocating it.

In this state of death the soul is purified by God. Unpurified emotional drives and feelings die, making room for Christ and thus for a pure, godly love towards our fellow-beings. In His desire to make us a vessel of His love, the Lord is concerned that our love should not blend with a tainted, soulish love, impure in its motives. The unpurified desires of our rational self, in which pride lies hidden, and the unpurified desires of the flesh also die. After such dying processes the love of God can place its divine imprint more fully on a person. God now blesses him, letting him delight in the sense of His presence as never before.

God leads us into this last kind of night with the aim of conforming us to His image. In other words, He wants His love to fill us and shine forth from us.

To attain this objective, it is not enough for Him to lead us into the night of chastening, where He deals with our sinful bondage and false emotional attachments. No, the process does not end there.

During the third region of the night God keeps on hammering at the soul till our own image disappears and our selfish, unpurified feelings and emotions increasingly die. He desires that all we think, say and do should be God-filled and that the only thing that stirs our hearts may be God in us. The apostle Paul writes of this goal: 'that according to the riches of his glory he may grant you to be strengthened with might through his Spirit in the inner man, and that Christ may dwell in your hearts through faith; that you, being rooted and grounded in love, may have power to comprehend with all the saints what is the breadth and length and height and depth, and to know the love of Christ which surpasses knowledge, that you may be filled with all the fullness of God' (Ephesians 3:16-19).

The light shining from the soul that has passed through the night is the light kindled by Jesus in the midst of darkness. This is achieved through the working of the Holy Spirit and through God's Word and Holy Communion. Just as the night sky reveals the glory of the moon and stars, so the soul reduced to nothing by spiritual night reflects the activity of the Spirit of God with greater clarity and purity than before. It is in the night that the most thorough purification process takes place; and this is why God leads all His beloved and chosen ones into the night. There they grow blind to themselves while their eyes are opened for God and His grace. They are no longer aware of showing love or doing good — a sure safeguard against conceit. When the person accomplishes good in spite of everything, then God alone is glorified.

During such times of night and dryness the spirit, too, is seemingly seized and tormented by death. Virtually paralyzed, it is scarcely capable of thinking about the things of God, let alone of praying with ardour. Just as the soul in this state loves God and its fellow-beings in the deepest, purest sense, though unconsciously so, for the person considers himself to be the greatest of sinners; the spirit undergoing night feels completely incapable of achieving anything — as if it had been put to death. Yet it is precisely then that it receives new thoughts and prayers inspired by God. Such a purified spirit has become a fertile ground for the Spirit of God; the divine power is made perfect in weakness.

According to eternal, divine laws, we have to undergo death. But those who have died to self here and now will not taste death in eternity: they will be spared the second death, for what has already died does not need to die again. Even in this life they will experience a spiritual resurrection with an outpouring of divine love, of God-given thoughts and inspirations. One could say that the night of chastening brings with it arrows to wound and pierce us, whereas the night with God overtakes us like an avalanche and nearly kills us. But to the same extent that the self-life in the realm of the soul and of the spirit dies, there is a new blossoming of life from God in its place.

How wonderful! One enters the night and finds divine life. One descends into hell, as it were, and finds oneself in heaven. So it is with the person who is led into the night with God. At first he has to accept having a dark cloud burst over him, raining down all kinds of suffering. If, however, he receives them in a spirit of love, the same cloud will send down upon him a stream of divine love.

This dark cloud accompanying the night with God can assume different appearances. Sometimes it can take the form of forsakenness and loneliness. This has nothing to do with the loneliness experienced in the night of chastening, the pain of being all on one's own and separated from others. Rather, it is a God-forsakenness similar to what Jesus had to endure, though with the difference that He bore it as the sinless One for our sakes. Even if we bear this forsakenness in the fellowship of His sufferings, it is still our due as sinners and necessary for our purification. We all know how agonizing loneliness and forsakenness can be. More people take their lives for this reason than for any other.

Loneliness is like a black hole of emptiness. It can drive a human soul to despair. Any other suffering would almost be preferable. Trials and temptations would at least mean there is a struggle going on; there is action. What makes God-forsakenness so hard to bear is that the person in his loneliness is in danger of being drawn into a state of death. Virtually paralyzed by the pain of forsakenness, he wants to cry out but cannot.

Loneliness comes like a murky stream. A sense of futility seeps into the heart, filling every corner. We are separated from all that is life — not primarily from people but from God Himself, who is the very source of life. When God withdraws from us, is that not death, since life is to be found only in Him (Psalm 104:29)? Is that not agony and desolation? Separated from Him, we are separated from the One who is love and the source of blessing and happiness. Without Him we feel as if we have been banished to a land of death, where nothing but emptiness and desolation stare at us and the soul nearly perishes in this waste. It is a hell-like condition. Such loneliness and God-forsakenness are perhaps the greatest ordeal of all.

Jesus endured all this for us on the cross in full measure, but even before Calvary He tasted it. Now He is allowing His chosen ones to partake of the fellowship of His sufferings. Because Jesus trod the path of loneliness and separation from the Father, we too can tread the path of God-forsakenness with Him, and we will find that this forsakenness will actually result in a holy fellowship with God. The holy Three in One comes to the lonely soul who in loving obedience has drunk the cup of loneliness to its dregs.

In the night of loneliness and desolation much is accomplished. Loneliness discharges its deadly poison, killing all soulish, selfish love. Nothing remains in the way of strength, power, virtue or righteousness. In the night faith has nothing else to cling to but the Word of God and the sacrifice of Christ. In the final analysis, faith hangs on the cross with the Lord. Everything is destroyed by the poison of loneliness, everything except the love of God, which is the antidote. The person who has the courage to withdraw for prayer, not fearing the loneliness, becomes aware of his inability to love, but at the same time he learns to draw upon the love of Jesus and so to love in truth.

In this night of loneliness much of the old self is put to death and a void is created. And now after the soul has endured aridity and the death of self, the wonderful moment comes for the Holy Trinity to come and dwell in this empty, afflicted soul. Without realizing it, the soul becomes a vessel of the Holy Trinity. Unnoticed, the Godhead quietly draws near in order to take full possession. For God, the high and lofty One, the holy Three in One, dwells 'with him who is of a contrite and humble spirit' (Isaiah 57:15).

We often assume that if the Holy Trinity is to descend to us we have to be aware of an ardent love for God, yearning for Him with all our hearts. Just the opposite is true. The way leads deeper and deeper into the night and forsakenness. When we think that our hearts are nothing but empty, dreary chambers rather like the dark interior of a cave, it is precisely then that God comes to the humbled person. Jealous for our love, He leads us into ever-increasing darkness and loneliness, so that our love dies to all else and we turn to God alone.

If we welcome this night and extol its benefits, we will discover that it is our loneliness which brings the Godhead closer. The void created by loneliness is filled by the presence of God in threefold fullness. We will still feel lonely and forsaken by God and man, but this will help us to concentrate on God alone. So we will experience heaven on earth. When we turn to the triune God, of our own free will deciding to live solely for Him, heaven comes down, and with it the Holy Trinity and an abundance of blessings. This marks the dawning of paradise in a person's life.

Let us consider Saint Francis of Assisi. Here was a man who turned exclusively to the triune God, having been reduced to nothing along pathways through the night; and the triune God drew near to him, letting him taste heaven. Henceforth he lived by the miracles of God. All the riches and blessings of God's creation stood at the disposal of him who had chosen poverty. When a person discovers the heart of the Godhead and his heart becomes a dwelling-place for the triune God, that man possesses heaven and earth, yes, everything, in and through God. Saint Francis of Assisi chose poverty and in so doing became rich; he forsook all and consequently he found that all the treasures of heaven and earth were his: the triune God and with and in Him all that belongs to Him, all that He created. He chose the depths of forsakenness and loneliness, and in so doing gained divine fellowship. The triune God came to live within him. This man of God was willing to die to all self-centred feelings and emotions, and an overflowing life of love and bliss was granted him.

O blessed night that gives birth to such tokens of grace! Hidden in its womb lie heavenly treasures, which it imparts even in this life to those who bear the darkness lovingly in gratitude to Him who bore the night of God-forsakenness for us. Do we now find it surprising that those who repeatedly undergo the darkest of nights with God are the happiest of all, scarcely being able to take in the wealth of the divine revelations with which they have been favoured? To them it is given to taste the peace of God and to enjoy His presence. They are visited by the triune God and granted the revelation of His glory. While in a state of hell and forsakenness, they live in the constant presence of God with their innermost hearts in heaven.

Truly, the way through the night is worthwhile. He who loses his life will find it. All that is needful for time and eternity, heaven and earth, is to be found in the triune God, the fullness of the God-head: Father, Son and Holy Spirit.

Father and Son enthroned on high,
The Holy Spirit ever nigh,
Eternal mystery surrounds God.
Silence majestic broods over space,
Cherubim praise the glorious grace
Of the three Persons but one God.

Out of the dark, a beacon flares,
And God's great holiness declares,
Fire of the Holy of Holies.
Love from eternity's source outpours,
Expressing holiness fire upsoars,
Uniting three Persons in One.

Here we have light, yet darkness too,
Holy our God, yet loving true,
Who can such mysteries fathom?
Holiness streams with brilliant rays
From round His throne, majestic the blaze,
Yet full of love beyond measure.

Trinity God — let all adore
Him who will reign for evermore,
Who in Himself is abundance.
Frail human souls who follow Christ's way,
Letting Him mould them day after day,
Will taste the rapture of God's love.

Like a great river streams God's love,
Filling all earth and heaven above,
That we may drink of its fullness.
Only this highest holiest place,
Hidden from sight and all earthly gaze,
Gives birth to new life and true love.

Other literature by
M. Basilea Schlink

A FORETASTE OF HEAVEN
(American edition: I FOUND THE KEY TO THE
HEART OF GOD)
Autobiography, 416 pages, illustrated
'Here I found Jesus, the living God, and not theory.
Here I discovered the heart of God, which weeps and
laments and overwhelms His children with love. The
secrets of a deep relationship of love for Jesus — far
surpassing my understanding — captivated my heart
and filled me with yearning for a deeper love for Jesus
and a closer walk with Him.'

REPENTANCE — THE JOY-FILLED LIFE 96 pages
A remarkable little volume, showing how an attitude
of repentance affects a Christian's inner and outer life.

THE CHRISTIAN'S VICTORY 192 pages
(American edition: YOU WILL NEVER BE THE SAME)
Prescriptions of 'spiritual medicine' for 45 different
sins. This intriguing book not only brings to light the
sins which mar the Christian's life, but it also helps us
to recognize them in our personal lives and points out
the remedy.

MY ALL FOR HIM 160 pages
'My life has changed completely since I opened my
heart to the message of loving Jesus first and foremost.
Never before have I experienced what joy it is to love
Jesus and how it makes everything else fade into
nothingness.'

STRONG IN THE TIME OF TESTING   96 pages

As Christians face growing pressures, the need to prepare for the testing of our faith is even more urgent than when these texts and prayers were originally written. We would never be able to bear the hatred, harassment and persecution in our own strength. Yet, as Mother Basilea encouragingly shares, in Jesus Christ we can find all the grace we need to stand the test of suffering. United with Him, we will experience the reality of Romans 8: Overwhelming victory is ours; nothing will ever be able to separate us from the love of God demonstrated by our Lord Jesus Christ when He gave His life for us.

THE ROYAL PRIESTHOOD   48 pages

In a perishing world crying out for help, messengers are needed who come from the presence of the living God — messengers who have been empowered by Him, reflect the glory of His countenance and truly are 'royal priests'. Today Jesus Christ, our great High Priest, is asking, 'Whom shall I send?'

GOD LAMENTS — AND OUR RESPONSE   64 pages

'I have discovered that when I am feeling very low and sorry for myself, reading and thinking about Jesus' sorrows makes me forget my problems and it really brings a joyful heart to know that I can bring Him joy.'

FRAGRANCE OF A LIFE FOR GOD   64 pages

A message for our times when countless offers to escape suffering, especially the cross of sickness, are coming from a wide range of groups (including those campaigning for 'death with dignity'). For everyone trying to discover the purpose to suffering and ways of coping, here is an answer tested amid the trials of everyday life.